PUFFIN ISLAND

by Ada and Frank Graham, Jr.
photographed by Les Line

COWLES BOOK COMPANY, Inc., New York

Roy and Wilbur asked that this book
be dedicated to their grandmother, Lottie Hutchins,
who taught them to love birds

CONTENTS

PART I
·
THE ISLAND

Captain Corbett peers into the fog around the *Audubon Queen*.

1

·

CAPTAIN PURCELL CORBETT OF CUTLER, MAINE, LEANED
on the rail of his sturdy boat and watched the three
figures walking toward him along the wharf. The boat's
engine thumped steadily below its deck, partly drowning
out the cries of the gulls that circled over the lobster
boats nearby. A thick fog was settling over the long
narrow harbor.

As the figures came closer Captain Corbett saw a
young woman dressed for wet weather and two boys
who seemed to be twins. They were carrying their
belongings in suitcases and small canvas bags. Binoculars
hung from leather straps around their necks. The woman
stepped carefully from the wharf onto the boat's deck,
which the wet weather had made slippery. Then the
boys handed their bags to Captain Corbett and dropped
onto the deck as lightly as if they had been around
boats all their lives.

"Throw off that line!" Captain Corbett called.

One of the boys quickly untied the rope that was
holding the boat's stern to the wharf and coiled it
neatly on deck. The engine roared as Captain Corbett
swung his boat away from the wharf. In a moment the
Audubon Queen was headed into the fog that drifted
landward from the open sea.

Aboard his father's boat, Roy measures lobsters to see if they are large enough to keep.

Captain Corbett's guess had been right. The boys were twins, Roy and Wilbur Hutchins, whose father was a lobster fisherman in a nearby coastal town. For the last few summers they had helped their father on his boat, which he had named after them—*Roy and Wilbur*. Although they had just turned eleven years old, they already knew a great deal about boats and the water and the things that lived in the bays where they fished with their father. But now the twins were setting out on a different kind of voyage.

After hauling a lobster trap aboard his father's boat, Wilbur throws back lobsters under the legal size limit.

"Would you like to go to Machias Seal Island with me?" Anne, a friend of their parents, had asked them several months before.

"Yes," Roy had said.

"Sure," Wilbur had said.

Only then had they thought to ask her where the island was. They had never heard of it, but it had sounded like an exciting place to visit. Anne, who had been there several times, was a biology teacher at a large university. She hoped to write a book about the island. She and the boys could explore it together, and perhaps learn many things that they might not learn alone.

"Are there seals there?" Wilbur had asked.

Anne had briefly described the island to them. Machias Seal Island, she had said, is simply a few acres of rock that rises out of the powerful tides and currents in the Bay of Fundy, nine miles off the coast of Maine. For a good part of the year the island is wrapped in storms and fog.

Even its ownership is wrapped in mystery. The island seems to belong to the United States through an old treaty with Great Britain. But years ago the Canadians took possession of it and built a lighthouse there because so many of their ships had smashed themselves to pieces on its rock sides.

Perhaps seals once rested or mated on Machias Seal Island. Today the seals are found only on a smaller rock a mile or so away. The island itself is inhabited only by the lighthouse keepers and their wives, and by colonies of seabirds that have found there the kind of privacy they need to nest and raise their young.

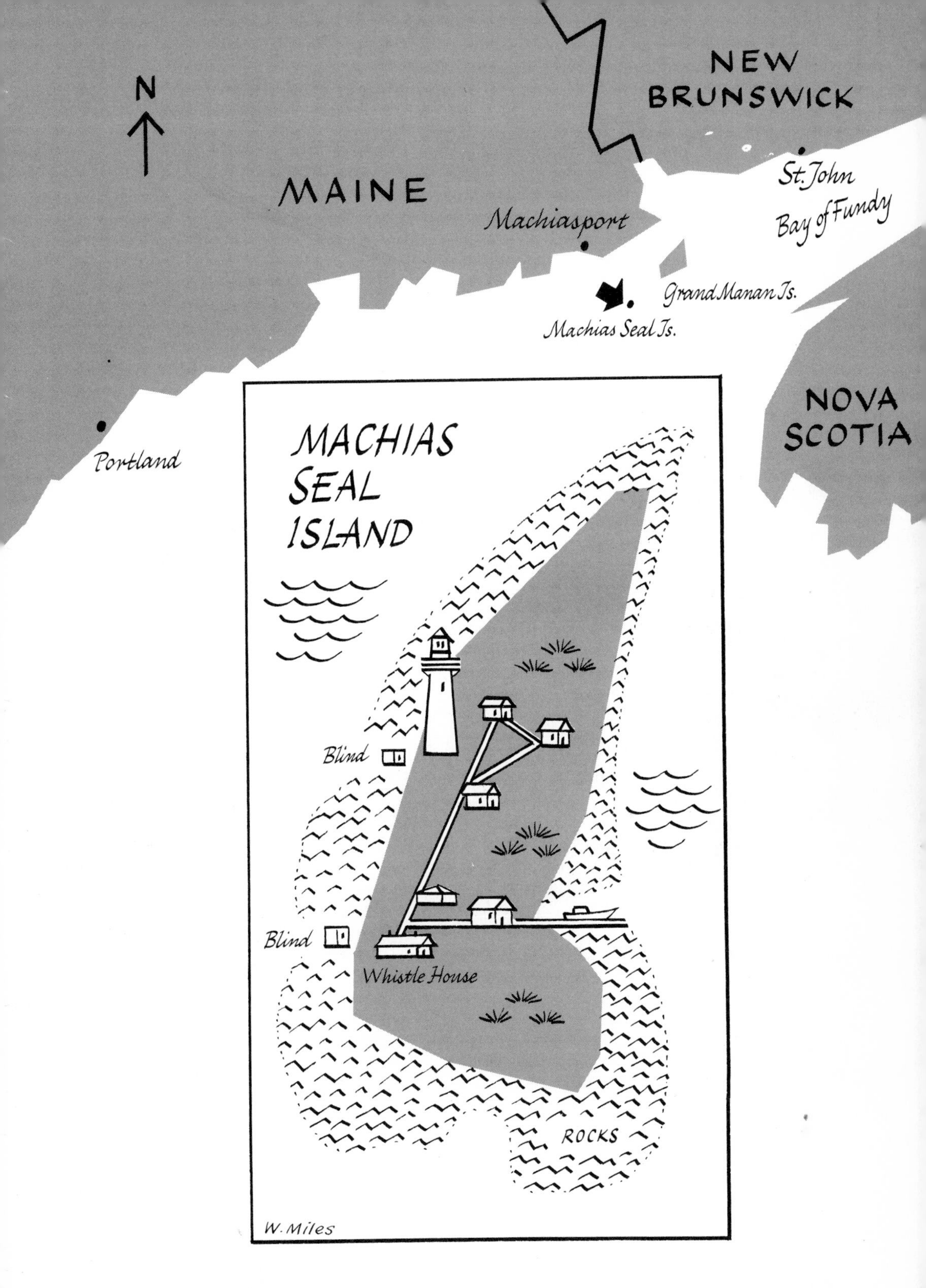

N

MAINE

NEW BRUNSWICK

Machiasport

St. John
Bay of Fundy

Grand Manan Is.

Machias Seal Is.

NOVA SCOTIA

Portland

MACHIAS SEAL ISLAND

Blind

Blind

Whistle House

ROCKS

W. Miles

It was then that Anne had told the twins a
island's main attraction—it is the nesting gro
sea parrot, or puffin. They would have the ra
opportunity to watch this unusual bird at close
and learn about its life.

Now Anne sat beside the twins as the *Audubon
Queen* left the mainland behind. A small empty
rowboat, tied to the craft's stern, bounced along in their
wake. Captain Corbett, who had agreed to take them to
Machias Seal Island, peered into the fog that still hung
low over the water.

There was a brief flurry of excitement when a round
black head was spotted in the gray water just ahead of
them. Roy and Wilbur leaned over the side, staring at the
creature, which looked for all the world like a small ape.
The creature stared curiously back at the boat and its
passengers. Then, just as the boat came alongside it, the
head sank from sight, leaving scarcely a ripple on
the water.

"Just a big ol' harbor seal," Wilbur said
matter-of-factly. He had seen many such seals while he
was out fishing with his father.

"I wish this darn fog would lift so we could see
something more," Roy said.

"You had better get used to it," Captain Corbett
told him. "They *make* the stuff down here."

This remark was intended by Captain Corbett as a
joke, but the boys knew that it had some truth to it:
the fogs of this part of the Bay of Fundy were famous
for the way they hung over the nearby coast for days at a

time. Roy and Wilbur began to worry that the fog would spoil their trip to the island. At this rate, they would not even be able to see the island from the *Audubon Queen.*

Here and there the fog showed signs of lifting. It seemed to be coming apart like an old piece of cloth. Roy and Wilbur were able to see farther now through the raggedy holes in what had been a dense curtain only a few minutes before. Suddenly they got their first clue that they were nearing the island.

"There goes a tern!" Anne called out.

The boys watched a slender, gray bird fly past the boat. It flew swiftly and gracefully on long, pointed wings. The boys seemed puzzled for a moment.

"What did you call it?" Wilbur asked.

"That's a tern—an Arctic tern," Anne told him. "You'll see lots of them on the island."

"We see those birds all the time back home," Wilbur said. "We call them mackerel gulls."

Anne nodded. "That's what the fishermen usually call them. They're related to gulls, but they're a different family altogether."

From the boat's rail Roy and Wilbur watched the terns. There were more of them now, diving for fish and screeching loudly in their excitement. The boys watched a tern flying near the boat. It stopped abruptly in midair, folded its wings, and plunged into the water with a sharp splash. In a moment it was back in the air, carrying a tiny silver fish crosswise in its blood-red bill. Wilbur turned to look for other terns, and there was Machias Seal Island.

A tern, carrying a tiny fish, flies out of the fog.

The *Audubon Queen* at mooring off Machias Seal Island.

They had come upon it through a break in the fog. The island was a low piece of land, resting like a rocky fortress on the sea. No trees grew on it, but in the center stood a cluster of neat white buildings, with the tall form of the lighthouse rising from their midst. The deep moan of the foghorn, which had been blotted out by the birds' cries, came to them now from across the water. Captain Corbett moved the boat in toward the shore.

"My gosh!" Roy shouted. "What's that?"

A plump little form had sped past the boat on rapidly beating wings. For a moment Roy had thought it was a small black and white duck. But no duck ever showed to the world such a beak as the bird that Roy had seen fly by. He had never seen anything quite like it before.

"That's a puffin," Anne said, laughing. "That's the bird we came to see. We'll get a better look at him later on."

Captain Corbett dropped the big anchor and the *Audubon Queen* came to a halt. The boys saw that there was no dock on the island, and that they would have to row to shore in the small boat. Working quickly, Captain Corbett pulled the rowboat alongside the larger craft.

"You boys jump in," he told Roy and Wilbur. "I don't want to take too big a load. I'll come back for the lady and your bags."

Several men were walking down a long steel structure that ended at the island's shore. This, Roy and Wilbur knew, was a boat ramp. The island's inhabitants used it to slide their own boats down from

the boathouse to the water. Captain Corbett
maneuvered them in close to the ramp. A gentle wave
pushed them the last few feet and, as Roy and Wilbur
looked up, helping hands were extended to pull them up
on the shore.

Captain Corbett rows Roy and Wilbur ashore.

2
.

"YOU BOYS BROUGHT GOOD WEATHER."

The man had a pleasantly wrinkled face and wore old work clothes over his lean frame. His friendly smile seemed to be a reflection of the late-morning sun that had just appeared through the scattering fog.

"For a minute I didn't think I was going to make it," Roy said. As the boat had bobbed in the watery swell he had made a leap for the ramp.

"That water's too cold to swim in," the man said, still smiling. "If you fall in here, what you want to do is grab hold of an anchor, and when you reach bottom run like heck for shore."

The boys laughed. This man had a comical way about him. Captain Corbett had returned now with Anne and their bags. He also handed up several boxes from the rowboat. They were filled with groceries—eggs, bacon, milk, fruit juices, bread, and several kinds of cereal. All of their food, except seafood, had to be brought to them by boat from the mainland.

"I'm Jack Russell," the friendly man said. "I'm one of the lighthouse keepers here. You can throw those bags on the wagon."

They piled their belongings on a flat wagon whose wheels rested on the rails that ran along the ramp.

15

Another one of the lighthouse keepers (there were three of them on the island, the boys learned) was standing at the top of the ramp. He started a winch that pulled the wagon up the ramp on the end of a steel cable. The boys jumped aboard for the ride.

On the way up they passed a sign that told them the island was a "Bird Sanctuary." As if to make it official, a tern sat calmly on the top of the sign, staring at them as they rode past. Other terns filled the air above them. ("As thick as flies around a garbage heap," Wilbur said.) Their cries were deafening.

This tern poses in a safe place.

At the top of the ramp Roy and Wilbur jumped off the wagon and looked curiously around them. They were in the boathouse, where the lighthouse keepers stored their small boats, oars, and outboard motors. Next door was the oil shed, where fuel oil to run the island's furnaces and machinery was kept in large tanks.

"And this is the whistle house," Jack Russell said, leading them into another building. "This is the machinery that makes the foghorn work. The diesel engines supply power that builds up air pressure to blow the horn. There are actually *two* horns—a short one that we call a blast, and a long one that we call a grunt. The grunt boosts the sound out over the water."

Because there was still some fog around the island the horn kept sounding regularly: it gave two blasts separated by five seconds, then a silence of fifty seconds, and then two more blasts.

"Each foghorn is different," Jack explained. "A foghorn on another island or point of land somewhere across the bay will have a different length of time than this one does between sounds. That way, a ship's captain can count the seconds between blasts, and know for certain which island he's close to. Then he can avoid the dangerous rocks nearby that the foghorn is warning him about. Get it?"

Roy and Wilbur said they got it. The foghorn did not seem terribly loud to them as they stood off to one side of the whistle house. But it was a different matter when they walked around to the front and stood directly in front of the widemouthed horn. When the horn blew at close range it sounded like a long, drawn-out cannon

17

blast. The boys ran around the edge of the building laughing, their hands pressed to their ears.

"It actually *hurts*," Roy said, sticking a finger in his ear and vibrating it rapidly.

"Yep," Jack said. He thought the boys' discomfort was very funny.

From the whistle house the boys could look up the island a hundred yards to where the lighthouse stood. Grouped around it were the three houses where the lighthouse keepers lived with their wives. Jack led the boys along a boardwalk raised above the level of the neatly clipped lawns. Wilbur stopped at the sight of a flagpole from which flew a strange red and white flag with a red maple leaf in its center.

"Gee, I never thought of that," he said, excited by the idea. "We're not in the United States now, are we?"

"No," Jack said. "We're all Canadians here. The Canadian government runs this lighthouse."

They stopped in front of one of the houses, which Jack said was his. Like the other two houses, it was fronted with clapboards, painted white, and had a red-shingled roof.

"We'll leave the bags here in front for a few minutes," he said. "You're going to stay with me and my wife while you're on the island. But first let's go up to the top of the light and look around while you still can see. Things happen so fast around here, they say that if you don't like the weather, just wait for ten minutes and it will change."

Anne and the twins followed Jack along the boardwalk to the lighthouse. Roy and Wilbur tilted

Jack Russell shows the island to the twins from the lighthouse platform.

their heads back to look up its whitewashed concrete sides toward the top.

"It's sixty feet high," Jack said. "Almost ninety feet above sea level, though, because the island is twenty-eight feet high at this point. Let's go up."

They walked inside through a door at the base of the tower. To reach the top they had to climb a series of iron ladders. Finally they came to the light itself, which was a huge bulb surrounded by lenses for casting the glow out over the water.

"That's a thousand-watt bulb," Jack told them. "I guess it would give you enough light to read by."

"I guess so," Wilbur said, grinning.

"Where do you get the electricity for it?" Roy asked.

"We generate all our own electricity here on the island with diesel engines," Jack said. "There's a motor that drives the lenses in a circle around the bulb. The light can shine through only some of the lenses, and that makes it look from a distance as if it's flashing off and on every three seconds.

"It's just like the foghorn, don't you see? If a captain doesn't know exactly where he is, he can tell which light he's near by the kind of flash it gives. You can spot this light fourteen miles away on a clear night."

Jack led Anne and the twins outside onto a platform that ran around the outside of the tower, high above the ground. The fog had almost disappeared and they had a fine view of the island and the sea around it. The island, they saw, was about three hundred feet across and a thousand feet long, curving away into a slender "tail" at its northern end. Beyond the tail was a tiny barren island called Gull Rock.

Part of the debris cast up on the island by heavy storms. Gull Rock
is in the background.

"That's where the sea gulls nest," Jack told them.

Machias Seal Island itself has a rocky rim. On the southern end of the rocks are great cubes of granite, tumbled one upon another. Though there are no trees growing on the island, its center is covered by a thick growth of grass and weeds.

Birds were flying everywhere. Roy and Wilbur said it gave them a queer feeling to be able to look *down* on flying birds, just as you would look down into a pool of fish. Farther down still, they could see some of the birds landing in the weeds. Others suddenly appeared out of the weeds and took off.

"Those are mostly terns," Jack said, pointing to the flying birds. "They make their nests in the weeds, or sometimes on the rocks close to the weeds. The puffins nest *under* the rocks, but there aren't many of them around now. They're out catching fish, or loafing on the water. There's a 'raft' of them floating on the water over there."

Roy and Wilbur turned their binoculars on a group of birds sitting on the water off the western edge of the island. The birds were still too far off to be seen clearly.

"You'll get a closer look at them later," Jack promised. "Let's go over to the house."

They went down the steep ladder and followed Jack to the house. Roy and Wilbur had somehow gotten the idea that they would be living in a glorified shack on this remote island. Instead they were pleased to discover that they would be living in a tidy modern house, with a bathroom, a furnace, tile floors—even a TV set! They were also pleased to discover that Jack's wife, Rita, was as friendly as he was.

"Make yourself at home, boys," she told them. "We've got everything here you've got in your own home, except lots of water. We get some water brought out to us in tanks by the boat that supplies all the Canadian lighthouses, but it's not very much. The rest of the water we collect is rainwater that rolls off the roof into a cistern. So take it easy on the water—*please*."

Lighthouse keeper Jack Russell.

Rita Russell showed the boys their room. They unpacked swiftly, placing their clothes in the drawers of the dresser, and the books and games they had brought on top of it. Then they washed their hands, using as little water as possible. The smell of fish chowder cooking on the kitchen stove put an added urgency into their preparations. By the time they entered the kitchen-dining area, their bowls of chowder were already on the table.

"This is good haddock," Roy said, tasting the fish in his chowder. "Where do you get it from?"

"Fishing boats come in here to anchor all the time," Rita said. "Like the one out there now."

Roy and Wilbur looked out through the kitchen window. Where the *Audubon Queen* had ridden at anchor only a few minutes before there was nothing in sight but a dark blue fishing boat.

"That's from Grand Manan," Wilbur said.

"How do you know where it's from?" Rita asked. "Grand Manan is a Canadian island."

Wilbur looked faintly embarrassed. "My daddy taught me the different ways people build their fishing boats. This one has a higher deck than the kind we build at home. That's the kind they build at Grand Manan."

"Well, you're right, young man," Rita said. "That boat *is* from Grand Manan."

"I'm glad I'm not in *their* class," Jack said, pointing to Roy and Wilbur. "I'd be at the foot of it."

"Eat up, fellows," Anne said. "It's time to explore the island."

3

.

It was not easy to walk around the island in June.
Beyond the lighthouse and the other houses to the north,
the boardwalk ended abruptly. Anne and the twins
found themselves walking along a spongy narrow path
that wriggled through dense weeds. All three wore
rubber boots. Wilbur carried a net that was attached to
a long, stout handle. Immediately, there was a *whoosh!*
and a harsh *kak-kak-kak!* made them duck with a
sudden start. They had invaded the territory of the terns.

"Put something on your head, boys," Anne called
above the racket.

Roy and Wilbur knew now why she had insisted
they wear caps on their explorations of the island. The
terns nested among the weeds. Anyone who set foot on
the path through the weeds they took to be an enemy.
To protect their eggs they dove with harsh cries at the
human beings.

"Ouch!" screamed Roy. He had been slow to put
on his old baseball cap and a tern had swooped down to
rap his skull with its sharp red beak. "That *hurts.*"

"You bet it does," Anne said, laughing at Roy as he
rubbed his cap in the place where it covered the bump.
"You're lucky it didn't break the skin." And then she
called out again, "Wilbur! Look out for the eggs."

Wilbur, startled, stopped and looked down. There were two small eggs, half the size of hen's eggs and speckled with brown, lying exposed on the path. Only a handful of tiny plant stems were placed around them, forming more the *suggestion* of a nest than a nest itself. Wilbur had nearly stepped on the eggs.

"Sometimes the terns lay their eggs in the open," Anne said. "Be careful where you walk."

"Boy," Wilbur muttered. "This is *work!*"

They continued down the path, three figures hunched over to guard against the diving, screaming terns, stepping carefully over and around the eggs in their path. As they arrived at the rim of rocks that circled the island, Anne stopped and pointed.

"Watch how the plants begin to change now," she said.

The boys squatted down for a closer look. "This looks like Queen Anne's lace," Wilbur said, touching one of the coarse-leaved plants through which they had been walking.

"Nope, it's called angelica," Anne said, "and it's a member of the parsley family. But you were close, because Queen Anne's lace is a member of the same family. They both have a cluster of small white flowers at the top. That's the way you can learn to identify things—by noticing ways in which they are the *same,* as well as how they're different."

"The flowers around here are *different*," Roy said, stepping down onto the rocks that led toward the shore.

"Right," Anne said. "Look, these plants are smaller, with fleshy leaves. They feel kind of rubbery,

26

Last year's angelica bent by the wind.

in fact. They're called roseroot stonecrop, and they have pretty little bunches of red or yellow flowers at the top. There isn't enough soil out here on the rocks for the bigger weeds like angelica to grow. So we get *different* kinds of plants, like this stonecrop that can grow in the little bit of soil you find between the rocks."

"The leaves are thick and rubbery like a cactus," Wilbur said, feeling them between his fingers. "It's funny they should be like cactus, that grows in dry places like deserts. It's usually wet here."

"But what kind of wetness?" Anne asked.

"Mostly salt water, I guess," Wilbur said.

"Sure. Land plants like these need *fresh* water to help them grow. The angelica and other plants are thick up there where there's lots of soil because the soil holds the moisture. But here on the rocks there's very little soil in the cracks and it dries out quickly. So perhaps, when fresh water comes, these stonecrop store up the water in their fleshy leaves so they'll have it when they need it—just like a cactus plant. Get it?"

"I get it," Wilbur said. It seemed reasonable enough to him.

"Closer to the water there aren't any plants at all," Roy observed.

Anne raised her eyebrows. "Oh, no? Look again."

Roy and Wilbur looked around them. Then they looked at each other and shrugged. They didn't notice anything, except that the terns had stopped diving on them once they had left the weeds where most of the nests were located. Suddenly Roy squatted down and ran his fingers over a golden mat that covered a rock.

"Is *this* a plant?" he asked.

28

Anne nodded. "That's lichen—golden lichen. It's a tiny plant that's really *two* plants in one—a fungus and an alga. They live together because it's easier that way. The fungus supplies the water and the minerals, and the alga manufactures carbohydrates. They get along fine like that."

Roy and Wilbur were down on their hands and knees now, looking through their hand magnifying glasses at the thousands of tiny plants that made up the golden mat on the rocks.

"You'll see lots of other different-colored lichens growing on rocks around here," Anne said. "And back home you'll find them growing on trees."

"I always called them moss," Wilbur said.

"So now you've learned something," Anne said.

Wilbur agreed that he had.

They were still a considerable distance from the water. The tides in the Bay of Fundy are the greatest in the world. There is a difference of forty or fifty feet in the level of water between high tide and low tide at some places in the bay. Here at the island the water level had dropped twenty feet at low tide, uncovering many rocks that spend the rest of the time under several feet of water.

"Let's go down and see what we can find in the tidal pools," Wilbur said. He looked forward to using the big net he carried.

Their progress over the rocks was slow. At each step there was something new to see. A dead gull had been washed up on the rocks. Lying on its back, with its wings partly spread, it looked to the boys like the carved eagles one sometimes sees on old buildings.

29

A young herring gull lies dead on the rocks.

A little farther along they came across a rusted bedspring wedged under a huge boulder.

Wilbur tugged at one end of the bedspring.

"How do you suppose it got under there?" he asked.

"The waves must have done it," Roy told him. "Nobody could lift a rock that big. The waves must have pushed the rock on top of it."

There were a hundred things to see on this strange shore, and there was a question to be asked about each of them. Roy turned over a rock and the earth beneath it was covered with sow bugs, or wood lice.

"Where do you suppose *they* come from?" Roy asked.

"That's a good question," Anne said. "How do you suppose they got out here to this island?"

"They probably floated out in some rotten old log," Wilbur guessed.

"Yeah, that's what *I* said," Roy added, kicking the rock back on top of the sow bugs.

"Good guess," Anne said. And they walked on.

They came to the place that the water reaches at high tide. It was marked by rockweed, a slippery, shiny seaweed with little bladders that were filled with water and went *pop!* when the twins stepped on them. The rockweed covered the rocks and hung over their sides like curtains.

The boys picked their way carefully over the slippery stuff, sliding gently off a rock instead of jumping when they had to drop down to a lower level. They reached a large tidal pool—a depression in the rocks filled with water. The retreating tide had left the rocks around it high and comparatively dry.

The boys were familiar with tidal pools. They had explored them at home and knew just how to go about looking for the fascinating creatures that they hold. When they stepped into the pool they poked about under the rocks and pulled out many tiny crabs. They lifted the curtain of seaweed and pried periwinkles and other small mollusks off the rocks. Wilbur swept his big net through the water and brought several fish, each two or three inches long, to the surface. By the sharp spines that grew on their backs the boys knew the fish to be sticklebacks.

Acres of seaweed are uncovered when the twenty-foot tide of the Bay of Fundy recedes. Wilbur and Roy investigate a tidal pool for marine life.

Wilbur displays strands of a kelp called devil's-apron.

Roy uses a magnifying glass to get a closer look at a sea urchin, a small marine creature with a thin, brittle shell covered by sharp spines.

"Here's a Chinaman's hat," Roy called, pulling a small shell off a wet rock. "I never saw one so big."

Wilbur and Anne looked over the mollusk, which the boys called a Chinaman's hat (because of its shape) and which Anne (a professor, after all) called a limpet. All agreed it was larger than any they had seen on the mainland.

Roy and Wilbur carefully looked over each of their discoveries. They peered at them through their magnifying lenses and felt the texture of their coverings. They played a game, trying to see how each creature defended itself against its enemies and against the sea. Some seemed to prefer hiding under rocks, others under the rockweed. The mussels tied themselves to stones to avoid being carried off by the surging waves. The Chinaman's hats simply clung to the rocks by suction and let the waves roll harmlessly over their streamlined shells.

"This fellow's got *no* enemies," Roy said, holding up a sea urchin he had found on the bottom of the pool. He was careful not to stick his fingers on the hundreds of long sharp spines that completely covered the half circle of its shell.

"Who'd want to eat him anyway?" Wilbur asked. "It would be like eating a porcupine."

"Lots of people eat sea urchins, especially in Europe," Anne said. "They're considered quite good."

"Let's see you eat *this* one," Roy said.

It was a little like a dare. Anne had seen other people eat them, spooning the meat out as one would remove the segments of a grapefruit. But she had never eaten one herself. This seemed a good time to try.

35

"Give me your penknife," she said to Roy.

She sliced through the sea urchin's spines and cut off the lower part of the shell. Then she gouged out the orange-colored meat with the knife blade and tasted it.

"Pretty good—if you like a fishy taste," she said. "Here, try some."

Roy made a face and turned away. But Wilbur, to prove he would try anything, took some sea urchin meat from the knife blade. It wasn't bad, he admitted. But, no, he did not care for a second helping.

The sea urchin (too tasty for its own good) was the only victim of the afternoon. All the other creatures were returned to their home in the tidal pool. In a little while the sea would cover the whole area, and life would go on in the pool as before.

"The tide's coming back," Anne called.

And so it was. Rocks that had been visible only a few minutes before were now sinking from view. The water, which twice a day rises and falls on the bay's great tides, was returning to claim its share of the island.

Anne and the boys gathered up their equipment and retreated higher on the rocks, where they turned to watch the sea's advance. A stiff wind had risen in the northeast. The waves rose and crashed against the outer rocks. The spray flew high in the air. The pool they had just explored disappeared in the boiling fury of the surf.

"Let's move back, Wilbur," Roy shouted above the roar. "Daddy said not to get too close to the surf."

As they walked back up the path toward the houses, they discovered that the terns were being distracted by another being. A small brown bat was trying to fly

36

Thirty-five-knot winds pound waves against the shore of the island.

across the open weed-covered ground, pointing for the shelter of the buildings. But the terns resented the bat's invasion of their territory. Diving and screaming at it, they tried to drive it out to sea. The bat, attacked by both birds and wind, was making little headway.

"Poor little fellow," Anne said. "He came all this way, and he didn't get much of a welcome."

The bat was the only mammal they saw during their five days on the island.

4

•

THAT NIGHT THEY SAT AROUND THE TABLE IN RITA
Russell's kitchen talking about what it is like to live on
an island. The sun still hung in the western sky, well
above the dark line of the mainland visible on the
horizon. The island was on Atlantic daylight time,
which is one hour ahead of eastern daylight time, and
Rita's clock said it was nine o'clock.

"There aren't many important events out here to
mark on the calendar," Rita was saying. "But one of the
big events of the year for us is the return of the puffins
in the spring. Then we know that it won't be long
before people come here, too, to see the puffins."

"Do a lot of big yachts come?" Roy asked.

"No, not many," Rita said. "There isn't a good
protected harbor here for boats to anchor in overnight.
And you already know that it's hard to land on the
island. That is, unless you've got someone who really
can handle a small boat, like Captain Corbett."

"We don't get many strangers coming up and
knocking on our door," Jack said. "That's for sure."

"Jack's right," Rita said. "People don't often take
us by surprise. If people want to come out here they
usually get in touch with someone like Captain Corbett
who knows these waters. We get all kinds of people.

The twins record Rita Russell's account of the puffins' arrival.

Some of them are scientists who want to study the birds. And some of them are bird watchers who just like to come and watch."

"How about you?" Jack asked the twins. "What are *you* doing here?"

"Well, we're here to watch," Wilbur said. "But we plan to study the birds, too."

"Think you'd like to live on an island?" Jack asked.

Wilbur thought for a moment. "It would be fun," he said. "But then there wouldn't be any other kids to play with."

"Our son will be out here soon," Rita said. "He can't stay here year round because there isn't any school. So he goes to school on the mainland."

"An island is a little like magic," Roy said.

"Why do you say that?" Rita asked.

"Oh, I don't know. It's just the way you come out here and there's nothing but miles and miles of water— and then all of a sudden this island comes up out of nowhere."

"There's a reason why an island comes out of nowhere," Anne said. "Islands are made in all sorts of ways.

"Some islands are built by volcanoes. The volcano erupts and spews out lava, and builds the island up from the ocean floor.

"Some islands are built by tiny animals called coral. These little animals come together in colonies. They die and leave their shells behind. Finally billions of these shells build up to make an island.

"But some islands didn't have to be built up. They were there all the time, like this island. It used to be a mountaintop on dry land. But then this part of the coastline sank, and the ocean rushed in and covered all the lowlands around it. Only this piece of land—this mountaintop—was tall enough to stay above water. It became an island."

"See what you learn if you pay attention," Jack said, grinning. "Even *I* didn't know that."

"Is there lots of snow in the winter here?" Roy asked.

"We don't have to worry about snow," Jack told him. "The wind is so strong it sweeps the snow off the island as soon as it falls."

"The pesky thing is salt," Rita said. "The storms blow so much salt water up against the houses that the salt sticks on the windows. Sometimes it gets so thick you can't even see out. Then you have to go outside and wipe it off."

"It must get awfully lonesome," Roy said.

"Well, we've lived on islands all our lives," Rita said. "We were born on Grand Manan Island just to the north of here. We've got our television set. And we've got a radio—one that *we* can talk over."

"That's a 'citizen band' radio, isn't it?" Wilbur asked. "My big brother's friend has one in his car."

Rita nodded. "That's right. We can use it to talk to some of our friends on the mainland because they have them, too. And every morning I talk to Captain Corbett. I tell him what he can bring me from the store, and he tells me who he is bringing out with him on his boat."

"Do many people come out here to stay with you?" Wilbur asked.

"Most people only stay the day. They go back

with Captain Corbett late in the afternoon," Rita said. "But some people stay with us for a few days—mostly scientists. We tell them things we know about the island, and they tell us things *we* didn't know.

"There was a botanist—a man who studies plants—who came here last summer. He told me he found one hundred and four different kinds of plants on this island. Why, there hardly appears to be more than a dozen if you don't know what you're looking for!"

It was very still on the island. Even the seas had quieted. Everybody sat and listened to the silence for a few minutes. Then Roy spoke.

"Will the foghorn blow tonight?"

"Not unless there's a fog," Jack said. "Of course, sometimes it seems like it never stops. There was one month—July—here a couple of years ago when the foghorn was turned on for six hundred and eighty-seven hours. That's a lot of fog, when you figure there were only seven hundred and forty-four hours in the whole month."

Jack was silent for a moment, thinking about something.

"Sometimes a ship comes close to the island and doesn't seem to hear the foghorn," he said at last. "One day earlier this year we had a real thick fog. I just happened to look out that window over there and all of a sudden I saw a big freighter coming right out of the fog at us. It was only a few hundred feet off the island.

"The other lighthouse keepers saw it, too. We were all running around outside trying to get a look at the freighter to see if there was something wrong with her.

43

The steam-powered foghorns that alert passing ships to the island's rocks.

Rita poked her head out the window and asked:

" 'What are you looking at—a bird?'

"I had to laugh. 'That's no bird,' I shouted. 'That's a lost ship!'

"I ran back in the house and turned the radio on. I'd seen the ship's name through my binoculars, so I called it out.

" 'You're about to go aground on Machias Seal Island,' I shouted into the microphone. 'Bear hard to your left!'

"It was a Greek freighter and I don't know for sure that they heard me. But anyway they turned away just before they would have gone on the rocks. Then the ship just disappeared into the fog and we didn't see it again."

Rita had cleared the dishes from the table. Jack stood up and stretched.

"Well, I've got to go on duty," he said. "That means I have to sit in the whistle house and keep an eye out for fog. But it's a clear night, and I don't think we'll have any."

"Let's go outside and see what's doing," Wilbur said.

Anne and the boys went outside and stood on the boardwalk in front of the house. The sun had set, leaving only a dull glow in the west. But the birds were still active. Roy and Wilbur could see their forms—the slender, graceful terns and the stubby puffins—flying here and there against the night sky. The ocean looked black and cold. The island, over which the lighthouse shed its strong beam, was a tiny point of brightness in all that enormous dark.

Thousands of terns hover over their nesting area as the sun sets on the sea.

PART II
•
THE BIRDS

Puffins by the dozens bask in the morning sun on Machias Seal Island before flying out to sea for a day's fishing.

1

.

"I CAN'T WAIT TO SEE THOSE PUFFINS UP CLOSE."

Wilbur had just finished a big breakfast of apple juice, cereal, bacon and eggs, toast, and milk. Roy, who had been slower to get out of bed, was trying to catch up.

"Tell us about the puffins, Rita," Anne said. "Do you ever see them around the island in the winter?"

Rita shook her head. "No, never. I always try to keep track, and the earliest we saw them was on April 10. They appear about the same date every year."

"What was it like?" Anne asked. "Did you just wake up in the morning and find them already on the island?"

Rita shook her head again. "Oh, no, they don't come right in. They always stay offshore for a few days first—almost like they're scouting the island. We looked out about nine o'clock in the morning and saw this big raft of birds on the water. Each day they got a little closer."

As Rita spoke, Roy and Wilbur felt the presence of puffins everywhere around them. They could look out the window and see the puffins standing on the rocks near the shore, or flying overhead. In the Russells' living room, tiny wooden puffins that Jack had carved and painted during the long winter stood on all the

51

tables. He sold them as souvenirs to people who visited the island.

"The puffins stayed offshore for about a week," Rita was saying. "Then, about nine o'clock one morning—I have it here in my notebook, it was April 18—this great cloud of birds appeared over the island. Oh, it was a beautiful sight to see, I can tell you. There were over twenty-five hundred birds and they all arrived at the island at once! They all came down on the rocks at exactly the same time!"

"Did you notice how they decided which bird was to get the best place to nest?" Anne asked.

"Oh, it was comical! They *fight*. It's really a show because they walk around on the rocks and scare off the next fellow. It's as if they are saying, 'You *move*. This is my territory.' "

"Are there any baby puffins born yet this year?" Wilbur wanted to know.

"Mammals are *born*, birds are *hatched*," Roy broke in.

Wilbur ignored him. "Are there any baby puffins born yet?" he asked again.

"Nobody has seen any yet," Rita said.

It was time for the twins to go out and see the puffins for themselves. They gathered up their binoculars and bird books and notebooks. They remembered to put on their caps, too. They would have to cross the grassy area where the terns nested.

High on the rocks above the western side of the island stood two *blinds*. These were small wooden buildings just large enough to hold three or four people. Instead of glass windows, the blinds had squares

A blind hides the boys from the nervous birds.

of burlap with small holes cut in them. People who wanted to watch the birds went to the blinds, where they remained quiet and looked out. The birds soon forgot that they had seen anyone enter the blinds and moved about unafraid on the rocks only a few feet away.

Anne and the boys ran for one of the blinds. Terns dived and screamed at them as they crossed the grassy place where they nested. One tern jabbed Roy on the top of the head. But he had his baseball cap on and it didn't hurt him. They entered the blind and closed the door.

In a few minutes puffins began to settle down on the rocks near the blind.

"Oh, here's one right outside!" Roy whispered.

"Let me see," Wilbur whispered, moving over to Roy's side of the blind.

"You don't have to whisper," Anne said. "Talking doesn't seem to bother the birds. But they get frightened when they see a sudden movement in the blind."

Puffins, alone or standing in groups, covered the rocks around the blind. They were very close, and Roy and Wilbur were able to see exactly what they looked like.

Perhaps because so many of its movements have a human quality, a puffin seems larger than it really is. It stands less than a foot high. The feathers on the bird's face, chest, and belly are white, darkening to gray near the edges. Black feathers cover the back of its head, and form a black "collar" around the throat. Its webbed feet are a bright red. Someone has described the bird this way: "The puffin looks like a rich old man in a dinner suit, complete with black jacket, white shirtfront, black bow tie, and a very red nose."

It is this "nose" that receives so much notice. Seen from the side, the puffin's beak is shaped like a heart lying on its side. The base of this beak runs from the forehead all the way to the chin. It is colored partly a bright fire-engine red. The rest is a kind of bluish gray and pale gold. A wrinkled orange "rosette" of flesh separates the bill from the puffin's face.

A puffin leans forward into gusting winds to keep from being blown away.

Two puffins pass the time on the rocks above their nests.

The puffin's eyes complete the picture of a sad-faced clown. The eyes have black pupils surrounded by a rich red color. Curious leathery plates above and below the bird's eyes gives its face a look of sadness.

The boys watched the puffins fly in from the water. The birds' wingbeats were short and very rapid, almost a flutter. Their red legs, webbed toes closed, trailed behind them. Then, as the puffins turned in flight, they spread their toes wide, using their feet on each side of the tail for extra rudders as they glided in for a landing. They steadied their wings, stretched their feet out toward the rocks below, and landed with a bump.

Some puffins, when they had landed, squatted so that they looked almost like ducks at rest. But other puffins stood up straight like penguins. All of them were very alert. They did not like to miss anything, and so they watched what their neighbors were doing. One puffin stood up on its toes and flapped its wings, then settled back down again. Another opened its mouth wide to yawn.

"Oh, look how yellow the inside of his mouth is," Roy said.

Once in a while a puffin would grab another bird's bill in its own. They wrestled with their bills. Then their neighbors would walk over to see the squabble (which never lasted very long). The puffins looked slightly bowlegged when they walked, their bills resting on their chests. But sometimes a bird walked past its neighbors as if it were showing off. Then it tried to look tall, holding its head and bill high.

Razorbills congregate by themselves on cliffs above the sea.

At high tide the water would be only a few feet below the birds.

"They look like penguins," Roy said. "Are puffins related to penguins?"

Anne was about to answer when Wilbur spoke suddenly.

"Jeepers, what's that?" he asked excitedly. "That's not a puffin. That bird over there *looks* something like a puffin, but it's different!"

Anne looked at the bird through her binoculars. Its color was much the same as the puffin's, though dark brown instead of black. But its bill was thinner, smaller, and jet black. The bill was marked with white lines.

"That's a razorbill auk," Anne said. "The razorbill is a relative of the puffin, but the *penguin* isn't really related to either of them. Here, let's look in some of our books and learn something about their history."

The history of these birds, the boys learned, is almost as colorful as the birds themselves.

2

·

WHEN THE FIRST EUROPEAN FISHERMEN LANDED
on the northern islands off the coast of the New World
in the sixteenth century they found some large
black-and-white birds that could not fly. They had
round white spots on their faces. The Europeans called
these birds *penguins,* which means "white head" in
Welsh. Here is how one of the early explorers described
these birds:

"These penguins are as big as geese, and fly not.
And they multiply so upon a certain flat island that
men drive them from there upon a board into their boats
by hundreds at a time; as if God had made the
innocence of so poor a creature for the benefit of man."

They were the first birds to be called penguins.
Later other explorers found birds near the South Pole
that did not fly, and they called them penguins, too.
Soon only the birds at the South Pole were called
penguins. The northern birds came to be called
auks, which is an old Viking name.

The great auks that the explorers found on the
northern islands had no need to fly. Until the Europeans
came they had no enemies that they had to fly away
from. They used their wings for swimming instead.

61

They were strong swimmers and caught fish in the cold northern waters.

The great auks spent most of the year at sea, because that was where they found their food. They came to the islands only in the summer to nest and raise their young. European explorers and sailors began to visit the island regularly to catch the auks for food.

The birds were easily trapped on the islands because they could not fly. In any case, they were not afraid of men. They had never seen men before and did not recognize them as enemies. The men simply herded them aboard their boats like cattle.

In this way all of the auks on the islands were finally captured and eaten. The last two great auks were killed in 1844 by two sailors who beat them to death with clubs. Thus the great auk became extinct.

But there are other, smaller members of the auk family in the northern oceans. One is the razorbill auk. Another is the puffin. The people of northern Europe had killed these birds and taken their eggs for many centuries. But they took only a certain number of birds, leaving behind enough to keep a healthy colony alive. Explorers and sailors hunted them on the American islands, too. But the razorbills and puffins are able to fly, so some of them escaped.

Puffins and razorbill auks, like their extinct relative, the great auk, spend most of the year at sea. They too are built for swimming. They have short, stubby wings, which they use as a seal uses its flippers. That is why puffins and auks are not good flyers. They must beat their stubby wings very hard to

The razorbill auk in its immaculate black-and-white dress was one of
the first birds to be called a "penguin."

stay in the air, and so they do most of their traveling by swimming.

One student of birds has described the way in which razorbills swim:

The wings are moved together—flapped or beaten—so that the bird really flies through the water. In flight, however, they are spread straight without a bend in them, whereas in the water they are flexed at the joint. The wings are raised and brought downward again toward the sides in the same position in which they rest against the sides when closed. The razorbill can dive to great depths, swim for long distances, and remain on the water for a long time.

The razorbill's short wings seem hardly suitable for flight, but they are well adapted to underwater swimming.

The puffins and auks have few enemies on the water. They are able to dive and escape a hawk swooping down on them, or men chasing them in boats. Once in a while a puffin has been found in the belly of a large fish. But in general they are safe, surrounded by the small fish, shrimp, and other marine animals that they feed on.

It is when these birds come to land in order to nest that they are in danger. Puffins and auks nest on the ground, and they would be killed, and their eggs eaten, if there were animals and snakes in the area. That is why, far back in the mists of time, puffins and auks began to nest on islands distant from the mainland. Those islands were too far from shore for animals to swim to them. Only other birds could reach them, or insects and other tiny creatures carried to the islands on floating logs.

And so, for thousands of years, puffins and their relatives have come to the islands in spring. They come on almost the same day every year, just as though they had the date marked on a calendar. Scientists believe that the birds respond to the longer hours of daylight as the spring progresses.

At any rate, the birds remain off the island for some days and form pairs. The males court the females. An ornithologist, or student of birds, has described this early courtship of the puffins:

> They swim together in closely crowded ranks, rarely diving, for their thoughts are not on food. Individuals rise up in the water and flap their wings as if from nervousness. Again two males fight vigorously, flapping their wings and making the water foam about them. Two

others, possibly a pair, hold each other by the bills and move their heads and necks like billing doves.

At last the birds come ashore. On some islands the puffins dig burrows in the soft earth and the razorbills lay their eggs in cracks high in the rocky cliffs. But on Machias Seal Island the two kinds of birds often nest side by side under the big rocks that have been tumbled on the shore by the powerful sea. Puffins like to nest far down under the rocks. Razorbills usually nest closer to the light.

Neither the puffins nor the razorbills are noisy birds. (The puffin, when it "speaks," makes a deep groan or grunt, which many people say has an unpleasant sound.) These birds communicate with each other mostly by sign language. The puffin is well equipped for this, and uses its wonderful bill to get across what it wants to say. This is how the British ornithologist R. M. Lockley describes it in his book *Puffins:*

> When this bird wishes to attract the attention of its mate it turns its head upward with a jerk, like a man waving a flag. "I am here, take note! Do you see me?" the jerking seems to say. But if the bird is a stranger or a rival, the bill is held stiffly forwards and downwards, showing the colors frontwards towards the enemy: "Be careful— another inch nearer, and I shall attack you!"

The puffin is able to make itself attractive to its mate simply by opening its bill, which has a bright yellow lining inside. If it wants to show another male that it is peaceful, the puffin turns away its head.

66

Razorbills, their black eyes nearly invisible in their black heads,
"bill" near their nest.

Then the other bird cannot see the "angry" red of the bill and accepts the first puffin as a good neighbor.

The female lays only one egg and spends a great deal of time sitting on it deep under the rocks. She is able to keep the egg warm even on the coldest nights of a northern spring because her normal body temperature is so high that we human beings would think of it as a dangerous fever—108 degrees.

Sometimes the male puffin relieves his mate. Then she is able to go catch some fish for herself, or perhaps just take a bath. R. M. Lockley once watched a female and tells us about it:

> She landed on the water as puffins usually do, with a little dive of the head partly below the surface. She immediately started to bathe, with every appearance of enjoying herself. She lay first on one side and then on the other, exposing her white breast as she beat the water with her wings and created a fine shower bath which seemed to penetrate her ruffled plumage. Her actions caused her tubby little body to revolve on the water like a slowly spinning top. Now and then she paused and shivered, like a farmyard duck on a pond.

When the puffin chick is hatched, the parent birds busy themselves bringing it food. They must also be aware of their enemies at this time. Gulls often nest near colonies of other seabirds. Their own chicks hatch at about the same time and they must get lots of food for their hungry young. Gulls are not expert divers like terns, nor expert swimmers like puffins, so they cannot catch fish very easily. Anyone who has watched gulls around a garbage dump knows these birds like to get their food the easy way.

Gulls usually obtain food for their chicks in two ways. They chase smaller birds like terns and puffins and make them drop the fish that they are carrying to their own chicks. Or they try to kill the helpless chicks of the other seabirds. (If the parent puffins are not careful, gulls will kill and eat them, too.)

R. M. Lockley often saw gulls kill puffin chicks on islands off Great Britain. First, a gull would swallow the chick to soften it up, and then fly off to its own nest and spit it up so that its chicks could eat it. Lockley once saw a gull snatch and kill a puffin chick that had wandered too close to the mouth of its burrow:

> The gull made three attempts to swallow it whole, while two adult puffins looked the other way indifferently. Each time the gull failed it ejected the corpse, only to pick it up and try again, throat stretched and head jerking viciously. After several failures it stood over the body and yodelled angrily. Once more it gulped and failed, choking down black bits of puffin fluff.
>
> At the next attempt it got the puffin's head down into its throat. Violent jerks of the head and success seemed near. The meal was half swallowed, the legs and wings still showing, and the gull looked extremely uncomfortable. Moving a few paces away the gull stretched its neck and swallowed with brutish motions of the bursting gullet. Slowly the bill closed over the last leg and wing.
>
> The gull was now quite out of shape, the throat bulging in an ivory ball behind the head, which it turned this way and that and gradually screwed its

69

monstrous lunch toward the stomach. With all the
appearance of acute indigestion the gull sat down on a
little hill with eyes half closed and neck and feathers
puffed up like those of a sick bird.

Lockley went on to describe in his book how the gull
finally went over to its own chicks and spit up the dead
little puffin. But the gull chicks were not able to tear
up the puffin. The adult gull then swallowed the puffin
again, after another hard struggle, and walked away.
As Lockley wrote: "Evidently supper was not quite
prepared yet!"

But young puffins that escape the gulls grow
quickly. After about forty days there comes a time when
the adult birds stop bringing fish to feed their young in
the burrow. The *pufflings,* as the young are sometimes
called, are alone in the world. They remain in the
burrow, sometimes wandering about at night. During
this time they eat very little—perhaps a few leaves and
twigs around the burrow.

Then one night the puffling heads for the sea.
Lockley has watched it:

It walks quickly away from its burrow, moving
downhill, and as all slopes on the island lead to the
sea it is on the right course. There is no fumbling or
pausing at the cliff edge. Over it goes, into darkness
and space, and finding itself airborne, it flutters
down blindly. Perhaps it will strike a rock instead of
the sea. If so it does not appear to be badly hurt. Its
short wings have lessened the force of the impact,
and its cushion of breast feathers and down has served
as a buffer. It bounces from hard and soft surfaces
alike, and plunges into the sea.

The puffling knows how to dive by instinct, and soon is catching its own fish. It swims farther and farther from the island where it had pecked its way out of an egg only about ten weeks before. By the time it joins a group of other puffins for its first winter on the sea, it is beginning to look like a puffin.

The young puffin's parents, meanwhile, have changed a lot, too. They no longer need the bright-colored bill that they used during the courtship season to attract mates and warn away rival puffins. So the colors fade and part of the bill falls away.

"The bill had lost its shape and was ugly," Lockley writes. "Its comic but colorful appearance had changed to a stage of undress, as if the clown had stuck half-way in the act of taking off his false nose."

But by the next spring each puffin has a brand-new costume. It grows a clean set of feathers. The marvelous bill reappears, as large and brightly painted as before. The puffin is ready to return to the island for another summer.

It was always like this on the islands off North America until the Europeans arrived. The puffins had little to worry about except their age-old enemies, the gulls, and once in a while a large falcon.

Then men arrived in boats, carrying their nets, their guns, and their clubs. The huge *puffinries* disappeared from many islands. In 1833 John James Audubon, the great painter of birds, visited the islands in the Bay of Fundy. He said he found some puffins on them, "although not one perhaps now for a hundred that bred there 20 years ago."

Man, even when he did not kill the puffins and

As the island awakens in the morning, razorbills leave one by one for a day at sea.

razorbill auks himself, helped to wipe them out in other ways. The puffins had tried to escape destructive animals by nesting on remote islands. But those animals came to the islands aboard man's ships. Cats and dogs killed the puffins in their burrows. Rats ate their eggs. By the early years of the twentieth century puffins were nesting on only two islands off the coast of the United States. There were only a half-dozen puffins left on Matinicus Rock, and perhaps three hundred on Machias Seal Island, both off the coast of Maine.

But then laws were passed to protect the birds. Lighthouse keepers like Jack Russell guarded them against men and animals. By the time Roy and Wilbur came to the island, more than twenty-five hundred puffins were nesting there.

3

.

"LISTEN, THERE'S A BUNCH OF THEM ON THE ROOF!"

Roy giggled and turned around to peer through a large crack between the boards in the rear wall of the blind. He saw a puffin flying on rapidly beating wings over the rocks. As the puffin flew it rolled its body from side to side so that one moment Roy saw the white feathers of its belly and the next moment the black feathers of its back.

Despite its odd shape and short wings, the puffin is a fast flyer.

"He's going to land on here, too," Roy said.

Both boys giggled as the puffin landed with a thump on the wooden roof of the blind. They could hear the scraping of soft feet as the puffins that were already there scrambled to hold their positions. Once in a while a puffin would take off. Then the boys saw only its backside through the front of the blind as the puffin sped toward the water.

"Here's one with some *fish*," Anne said. She had been looking through a hole in a side wall of the blind. Both boys rushed for that hole to see for themselves.

Roy watches the arrival of a puffin carrying fish for its young.

A puffin with a beakful of fish.

"Holy cow!" Wilbur said. "He's right outside here—
and he must have about six fish in his mouth at once."

The puffin stood quietly on a rock near the blind.
It held the fish crosswise in its beak, the slender
fish drooping over the corners of its mouth like a
silvery moustache.

"How can he keep catching fish without letting all the others get away?" Roy asked. "You'd think the others would fall out when he caught the last fish."

"That's a good question," Anne said. "I don't think anybody knows for sure. Do any of those books there tell you anything about it?"

Roy and Wilbur opened several of the books on the board that served as a table in the blind. They looked in the index, and thumbed through the pages.

"Bent doesn't say anything about it," Roy said.*

"Here's something," Wilbur said. He was looking through R. M. Lockley's *Puffins*. "They think the puffin kills the little fish with one hard bite. He's got a strong hook on the end of his beak. Then he pushes every fish all the way back. The beak has sharp little spines pointing backward. They think the puffin keeps all the fish in with those spines and his tongue—even when he opens his mouth."

The puffin stood on the rock holding its fish. Suddenly it hopped to a lower rock, fluttering its wings, and disappeared into a hole between two other rocks.

"What do you think that was all about?" Anne asked.

Roy's face lit up. "He must be feeding a chick."

"Can we go out and see if we can find a chick?" Wilbur asked. The twins were excited by the sign that at least one puffin chick had already hatched on the island.

"Let's wait for Jack Russell," Anne replied.

* For a complete list of the books that Roy and Wilbur brought with them to the island, see page 138.

78

"He said he would find a puffin for us under the rocks. Maybe he'll find a chick, too."

The boys were getting restless, but they settled down to wait. There was still much to see on the rocks. Three or four razorbills stood quietly a little off to one side of the puffins. One of the razorbills yawned.

"Wow, look at the inside of his mouth," Wilbur said. "It's a brighter yellow than even the puffins have."

"See, the razorbill has something bright to show, too, when he is courting his ladylove," Anne said.

"They stand funny," Roy said, pointing at the razorbills.

"They walk funny, too," Wilbur said.

A razorbill does a comic dance step while walking on the round rocks. Unlike the puffin, the razorbill walks in a flat-footed fashion.

Wilbur, in the blind, makes notes on the bird's behavior.

The boys now had a good opportunity to compare puffins and razorbills because the two birds were close together. The puffins often stood up on their toes. They walked on their toes, too, and seemed to move about very easily, like ducks. But the razorbills both rested and walked on the entire lower part of their legs, or "feet." This made them look very awkward. It also prevented them from walking as easily and rapidly as the puffins.

"He looks like a man trying to walk on his elbows," Roy laughed.

Wilbur opened his notebook. While he was waiting for Jack he would make some notes on what he had seen from the blind. This is what he wrote:

We are at a bird sanctuary, studying birds for a book. The first thing I learned is that when you go near the nest the terns swoop at you to scare you away.

The puffins come in and sit on the rocks. You can talk in the blind, but don't stick your fingers out the holes in the blind because you will scare the birds on the rocks.

The puffin doesn't go at all as far out to sea as the tern. The puffin stays close to the water when it flies.

The puffins come in on the back side of us and knock one another off the blind. There were about 30 or 40 on the roof at one time. They stayed on the roof when we were making a noise. When the birds take off it sounds like the body is too heavy for the bird's wings.

The puffins seem to stay on the upper side on the island. There were at least 50 on the rocks in front of us. When a puffin goes off balance on a rock he

flaps his wings rapidly to stay on top of the rock he is
standing on.

The puffins glide in when they land on a rock
with their wings out.

The puffin has only one egg.

Wilbur stopped writing when he heard a terrific
uproar outside the blind. The terns were screaming as
loudly as if someone were stealing all their eggs.
But in a moment the door opened and Jack stuck his
head in the blind.

"Do you want to go look for a puffin?" he asked.

"Yeah!" shouted Roy and Wilbur. They had been
in the blind for a long time.

Jack led them out on the rocks in front of the
blind. He was wearing a pair of heavy work gloves.
The rocks were whitewashed with droppings where the
puffins had stood. The groups of puffins stood their
ground nervously for a moment. Then, as Jack and
the twins drew nearer, the puffins took off and flew out
over the water.

Jack stopped several times to look under a rock.
Finally he got down on his hands and knees and stuck
his long arm into a hole between two rocks. He drew his
arm out slowly and there, in his hand, he held a
handsome and kicking adult puffin.

"You better wear gloves when you handle these
little fellas," he said. "They can draw blood with these
claws. And don't let them nip you with that beak. That
would *really* hurt."

The boys, close to a puffin for the first time, looked
at it carefully. Wilbur ran his hand softly over the back
of the puffin, stroking its feathers, but Roy preferred

not to come so close. He had a great deal of respect for that colorful and mean-looking beak.

At close range the bird was more beautiful than they had guessed. They saw the deep red around its eyes. They noticed that the beak, which looked smooth from a distance, had several horny ridges on each side. And they noticed the tiny claws on the toes of its red webbed feet.

"Three toes," Roy said, counting.

"That's right," Jack said. "It doesn't have a fourth toe behind like lots of other birds have."

The puffin continued to struggle. Jack let the boys look closely at it once more, then set the bird down at the entrance to its burrow, and it scurried down into the hole.

"That's *his* adventure for today," Jack said. "He can tell the wife all about it."

Roy and Wilbur began to explore the rocks now by themselves. Anne followed them, bending down to see what they were pointing at under each rock. Wilbur discovered several more puffins, each too far back under a rock for him to reach. Roy saw a puffin's egg, gleaming white, deep in a hole under a large rock. An adult bird sat next to the egg.

"Gee, these mothers don't sit on their eggs much," Roy said. "Why not?"

"A puffin doesn't have to sit on its egg very often when it's close to hatching," Anne replied. "There is enough heat in the egg itself to keep it warm."

"Here's a funny-looking egg," Wilbur called. "Is *this* a puffin's egg?"

Anne and Roy went over and peered into the hole

83

Wilbur had found. They saw a bird sitting near the eggs with its back to the entrance. Roy hollered. The startled bird turned its head, and they saw by its bill that it was a razorbill. Its egg was not oval like the puffins' eggs, but narrowed to a point at one end. The egg was heavily spotted with chocolate brown markings.

This is all that's visible of Wilbur as he hunts for a puffin's nest beneath the rocks.

The single egg of the puffin is laid in a skimpy nest in a burrow or crevice in the rocks.

"Do you know why the razorbill's egg is so different from the puffin's?" Anne asked.

Roy and Wilbur thought and thought, but could not think of a good answer.

"Well, a puffin's egg is oval and white because puffins *always* nest in holes," she said. "If the egg rolls around a little down there, that's all right because it can't go anywhere. And it's always hidden in the hole from gulls and other enemies. So it doesn't make any difference if it is a color like white that's easy to see. In fact, it makes it easier for the big puffins to find down there in the dark.

"But on a lot of islands the razorbills nest in the open on cliffs. Their eggs are pointed, so if they roll, they won't roll very far and fall off the cliff. They'll probably roll in a circle—like a top does when it's lying on its side. And the blotchy color helps to hide it from the gulls that are flying overhead. The egg blends in with the ground."

Roy and Wilbur thought it over and agreed that it made sense.

"But it doesn't always work," Wilbur said. "The books say that the gulls get a lot of the eggs."

"Sure," Anne said. "A rabbit can run fast so as to get away from its enemies. Foxes catch a lot of rabbits, but enough rabbits are able to run away and so they don't become extinct. It's the same way with razorbills' eggs. The gulls don't notice all of them, and those are the ones that hatch."

There was a shout from Roy.

"Look, this egg is broken open—and something is moving under here!"

He was looking under a large rock. Wilbur squeezed in beside his brother and hung head downward to get a better view.

"Hey!" Wilbur shouted. "The chick is out!"

"Let *me* see," Roy said, trying to elbow his way back into a good position. "I can't see him. He's already moved back into a dark corner. There's nothing left but the broken egg."

Anne got down on her stomach and looked in.
She reached under the rock and slowly, carefully,
drew out a fluffy little ball of life. It was kicking
feebly. The boys could hear faint squeaks coming from
the fluffy mass.

"It's a baby puffin," Anne said. She smoothed its
downy feathers.

"My gosh, he doesn't look at *all* like a puffin,"
Wilbur said.

A day-old puffin chick.

"He looks like a little animal," Roy giggled. "Like a mouse that doesn't have a tail. He looks so different from his mother."

"Well, you've found the first puffin chick of the year," Anne told them. "That's something."

The twins looked at the chick as Anne held it cupped in her two hands. Its feathers were not yet developed, and they looked like silky fur. They were a dark brown or black, except for a spot of white on the breast and belly. The short, thin bill gave no hint of the wonderful showpiece into which it would someday grow.

"Look, it still has its egg tooth," Anne said, pointing to a tiny yellowish point on the end of the black bill. "The egg tooth falls off soon after the chick uses it to peck its way out of the shell."

"Then it must have been born today," Roy said.

"Probably," agreed Anne. "Seabird chicks look older when they're born than a lot of land birds that are born blind and helpless. These little fellows can see and move around just fine."

Both of the twins ran their hands over the chick's coat of down.

"I'll bet this keeps him good and warm," Roy said. Then he laughed. "Listen to him. He *sounds* like a mouse, too."

"He wants to go home," said Anne. "It's not good to handle these young birds too much. Now that we've had a good look at him we'll put him back."

She set the chick down under the rock. It scrambled back into the darkness where an adult puffin, probably its mother, was quietly waiting for it.

4

•

RITA RUSSELL BROUGHT A ROAST CHICKEN FROM THE oven and set it on the table for dinner. Jack stood up to carve it.

"Well, Rita, this is one of the fattest puffins we've had for dinner in a long time," he said.

"That's not a *puffin*," Wilbur said skeptically.

Jack nodded. "Sure it is. Where would we find a chicken around here?"

"Don't let him tease you," Rita said, putting some mashed potatoes on Wilbur's plate. "He's a great teaser."

"*We* know the difference," Wilbur assured her. "Pass the gravy, please."

Rita turned to Jack. "Remind me to call Captain Corbett on the radio—these boys are drinking up the milk fast, and he'd better bring us some more."

"How do you get your groceries in the winter?" Roy asked Jack.

"The Canadian Lighthouse Service has a big boat. They go around to all the islands that have lighthouses on them and drop off supplies—food, water, oil— everything we need."

"Why doesn't the United States have a lighthouse here?" asked Roy.

"I guess because they just never thought to put one up," Jack told him. "This island is on the sea route to Canadian ports, and so it was mostly Canadian boats that were hitting the rocks around here."

"But who *owns* the island?" Roy asked.

Jack grinned. "Nobody will say for sure. As long as the Canadian government keeps a lighthouse here the United States won't argue about it. We're helping to save *their* ships, too—and it's not costing the United States any money."

"And with people like Jack here, the puffins are protected, too," Anne said. "You know what we read today about how the puffins were driven off the other islands in this area. The puffins need *friends* like Jack."

"Rita is a friend of the puffins, too," Jack said. "Tell them about the visit you had last summer."

"Oh, my, wasn't that something?" she said, her face brightening. "Well, you know that after a while the adult puffins leave the chicks on their own. I suppose the young birds get sort of lonesome down there in the burrow. They like to come out at night and wander around. I guess they like to explore the island like Roy and Wilbur.

"One night last August I was here alone—Jack was on duty over at the whistle house. All of a sudden I heard a tapping at the front door. I looked out the window, but I couldn't see any light in the other houses, so I knew nobody else on the island was awake. And it wasn't likely there would be anybody just 'passing by' away out here.

90

"Then I heard some more tapping. I went to the front door and opened it. And, do you know what? There was a baby puffin standing there on the step! He just walked right in the house. He stayed for about half an hour, just walking around and looking things over, and then I let him out again."

"See what I told you?" Jack said, grinning. "Rita is the puffins' friend, too."

PART III

·

PARTS OF A
WORLD

Wings beating furiously, a female Arctic tern hovers like a helicopter before alighting on her nest.

1

·

Roy and Wilbur were watching an amazing show. They were in blind number two, closer to the lighthouse than the other blind from which they had watched the puffins. Near the blind two terns were moving around each other on a large flat rock.

"It looks like they're doing a dance," Roy said.

He was watching the terns through binoculars. One of the terns—the male, Anne guessed—had just flown in from the sea with a little fish in its thin red bill.

"That's a brit he's got in his bill," Wilbur said.

"What's a brit?" Anne asked. This time she was on the receiving end of information.

"That's what we call the young herring," Wilbur said matter-of-factly. "Now look!"

The tern began to walk around on the flat rock, still holding the little fish. It was behaving in a very curious way. Strange growling noises came from its throat. It stretched its long tail, pointing it toward the sky. There was no doubt that this tern was trying to impress the female tern, which was sitting on two eggs in the grass at the edge of the rock.

But the female pretended to ignore the other tern and its fish. The male kept on growling and strutting on the rock.

95

In this series of pictures a male tern arrives on the nesting ground to court his mate with a fish. The female, who has been sitting on the eggs, scolds the male (1). Then she ignores him and his gift as he bows and circles around her (2). Finally she acknowledges his offering (3) and accepts and eats the fish (4). In the last picture (5), the male stretches his head high in the air in triumph.

97

"What are they *doing*?" Wilbur asked.

"This is all part of the ceremony that the birds go through during the nesting season," Anne said. "The male is offering the fish to the female, but she's playing hard to get."

Finally the female got up off the eggs and walked over to the male. He walked around her, offering her the fish. But she kept on with her game. She turned her head the other way and refused to take the fish. Then, after several more offers by the male, she took the fish from his bill.

It was a grand moment for the male. He had won! He pointed his bill in the air, as if he were stretching for the sky. He was going through a victory dance.

"Ain't he *proud*, though," Roy said.

"What kind of tern is it?" asked his brother.

Anne opened the guidebook on birds to a page where terns' heads were illustrated in color. The boys looked at each of the pictures, and then looked out at the birds on the rock.

"I can't see for sure," Wilbur said. "Has he got black on the tip of his bill?"

"No, it's red all the way down," said Roy, who had the binoculars.

"Then it's an Arctic tern," said Wilbur. He looked at Anne to make sure he was right.

Anne nodded. "That's right. The Arctic tern and the common tern look almost the same. But the common tern's bill is not as red, and it has some black at the tip. So those are Arctic terns there. If we look hard, though, we'll see some common terns nesting around here, too."

98

A rare photograph of a female Arctic tern who is just leaving her nest and its two eggs to find food.

Anne and the twins had been reading about these terns while they waited for the birds to land with more fish. The Arctic tern, they learned, is one of the world's great travelers. It nests in the far north. Many of these birds migrate as close to the Arctic Circle as it is possible to and still find dry land for nesting. Then, when they have finished nesting, they fly south to spend the winter not far from the South Pole, a distance of many thousand miles.

There is good reason for the Arctic tern's yearly migration, which is the longest made by any bird in the world. In one sense the sea is just the opposite of the land: it produces the richest growth of living things in its colder waters. The Arctic terns manage to avoid the ice and storms of winter by always flying to the hemisphere that is enjoying summer. But they keep to the coldest waters of that hemisphere because there it is easiest to find a large supply of food.

This is what Roy and Wilbur read in A. C. Bent's *Life Histories of North American Gulls and Terns:*

The Arctic terns have more hours of daylight and sunlight than any other animal on the globe. At their most northern nesting site the midnight sun has already appeared before their arrival, and it never sets during their entire stay at the breeding grounds.

During two months of their stay in the Antarctic they do not see a sunset, and for the rest of the time the sun dips only a little way below the horizon, and broad daylight continues all night.

The birds therefore have 24 hours of daylight for at least eight months of the year. And during the other four months they have more daylight than darkness.

The Arctic terns, Rita had told the boys, arrive on the island in the middle of May. They leave in August. But many of the terns flying farther north do not reach their nesting grounds until the middle of June. Arctic terns usually stay longer in their winter home in the south.

"This leaves them scarcely 20 weeks for the round trip of 22,000 miles," the boys read. "Not less than 150 miles in a straight line must be their daily task, and this is probably multiplied several times by their zigzag twisting and turning as they look for food."

Wilbur and Roy had watched the terns fishing when they came out with Captain Corbett on the boat. Now they read an ornithologist's description of the process:

"Looking at the water with down-turned head and bill from a height of 30 to 40 feet, the tern falls with the speed of an arrow, strikes the water with a splash, and often disappears completely below the surface in order to capture its prey. As it rises from the water it shakes its feathers, and the fish may be seen hanging from the bill.

"Sometimes it throws the fish into the air either for pure fun or to get a better hold. Sometimes the tern drops the fish, but catches it again before it has fallen more than a yard or two. The presence of the fish in the bill never interferes with the ability of the bird to scream or cry out. In fact the tern generally screams constantly as if to announce its success in the chase."

Students of birds know what route the terns follow because they have *banded* them on their nesting

The beautiful Arctic tern was once killed for its feathers, used to decorate women's hats.

grounds. That is, they have put a thin aluminum band on each tern's leg. Every band has a different number and a record is kept of the date of banding, location, type of bird, and its size and weight. If the bird is later found—dead or alive—then the scientist can tell in which direction the tern moved. In 1917, for instance, a young Arctic tern was banded on an island off the coast of Maine. Four years later this tern was found dead nead the Niger River in West Africa.

Years ago the terns were hunted and shot for their feathers, which were used to make women's hats. The terns were almost wiped out on the islands along the Maine coast. But then laws were passed to protect them. In recent years the tern colonies have returned to the islands. The Russells believe that there are now four thousand terns nesting on Machias Seal Island.

The air seemed alive with terns' cries. Roy and Wilbur watched the birds fly in from the sea with their fish. They saw the strange ceremony repeated many times. Once they saw a tern fly in with *four* fish in its bill.

"He thinks he's a puffin," Roy said.

Anne turned her tape recorder on. When she played it back they heard that the recorder had picked up the high, sharp cries of the terns all around the blind.

"What would happen if we took the tape recorder outside?" Wilbur asked. "Maybe we'd pick up the bird sounds even better."

Anne shrugged. "I don't know. Why don't you take the recorder outside and see what happens?"

Wilbur and Roy carried the tape recorder outside. The terns seemed to double the volume of their cries when they saw the two boys. Roy held the microphone high in the air. Terns swooped at Wilbur's head, uttering their harsh *kak-kak-kak* as they came.

"Ouch!" he screamed, holding his hand over his head.

Roy was laughing so hard he could hardly hold up the microphone. "What did it *feel* like?" he asked between bursts of laughter.

A diving tern finds its mark—Wilbur's head.

The sky is filled with protesting terns as the boys walk through the nesting grounds.

"It felt like he sat on me," Wilbur said, laughing too. "Let's get out of here!"

The boys rushed back to the blind. Once inside, they played back the tape recording they had made out on the rocks.

"I don't hear anything," Wilbur said. "Except static."

"That's not static, that's the wind," Anne said. "The wind blows too hard across the island. You would need special equipment to pick up any other sounds out there."

Roy and Wilbur looked disappointed.

"That's all right," Anne said. "There's one interesting thing about making experiments like this. You learn something even when it doesn't work out."

"I'm learning to wear my baseball cap all the time," Wilbur said. He was still rubbing his head.

2
.

"ONE WITH ONE!"

"One with one!"

"One with *two!*"

The air rang, not with terns' cries, but with the shouts of Roy and Wilbur. The terns, in fact, seemed quieter than was usual when strangers were invading their nesting grounds. Perhaps they were just puzzled by the commotion that was taking place on the rocks below them.

Roy and Wilbur were making a count of the terns' nests. With Anne's help they had drawn up a plan to count all of the nests near the paths through the nesting areas and on the rocks that surrounded the island. They decided not to count the nests in the grass and weeds. The terns' eggs would be too difficult to see there, and they were afraid that they would step on them.

Roy and Wilbur believed that a nest count would give them a good idea of the number of terns nesting on the island. They would have to search for the nests in order to appreciate the island's importance as a *ternery*.

But they would do more than simply count nests. They would keep a record in their notebooks of the

107

Wilbur (left) and Roy count terns' nests among the island's tumbled rocks.

number of eggs in each nest—how many nests held one egg, how many held two eggs, and so on.

The boys separated in order to cover more ground. But to double-check figures they called out to each other the number of nests they saw and the number of eggs in the nest. That way, they should have the same figures in their notebooks when they were through.

"One nest with one egg!" was how they called to each other when the count began. But soon they shortened their calls: "One with one! One with two!"

"Some of them are hard to see," Wilbur said.

"You generally see a little hay lying around," Roy said. "And then you look closer and there are the eggs."

"How come the eggs are different colors?" Wilbur asked.

"I don't think anyone knows for sure," Anne said. "You would think that it has something to do with the color of the ground they are laid on. But sometimes two eggs in the same nest are colored differently. Look at the two in that nest—one is light green, and the other is darker green with brown spots."

"How do we know these are Arctic terns' eggs?" Wilbur wanted to know.

"We don't," Anne said. "You can't tell a common tern's eggs from an Arctic tern's. I'm sure they both have nests along here. But we know from seeing the birds themselves that most of them are Arctic terns."

"I don't know why they even call them *nests*," Wilbur said. "Half the time the eggs are just laid on the bare ground."

"Well, some birds don't make very complicated nests," Anne said. "Especially birds that nest very close

109

together, like terns. But you'll notice that they always put a few pieces of straw or some twigs around the place where they are going to lay their eggs. That's just to show that the place is theirs."

"Where's Roy?" Wilbur asked.

Just then Roy's head popped up from behind a large rock.

"One with one, Wilbur," he shouted.

"One right here with one," Wilbur called back.

"Wilbur, what are you saying?" Roy shouted. It was sometimes hard to hear with the terns calling and the wind blowing.

"One with one in it!" Wilbur shouted. "*Another* one with one!"

"Wilbur, I *got* that one already!" Roy shouted back.

"One with two!"

"Wilbur, I *told* you—I got those already. You're coming too close to this side."

"Here's three!" Wilbur called.

Anne and Roy ran over to look at the nest Wilbur had found. There were three small green eggs, blotched with brown, lying in it.

"That's the first nest with three we've found," Anne said. "Mark it down in your notebooks."

They went on with the count. They found nests in shallow cracks between rocks. They found them partly hidden under tufts of grass. And they found a nest, with a single egg in it, lying on the rotting wreck of a small boat.

"There's two up here with one in them," Roy called. "Did you get them two, Wilbur?"

How many terns' nests can you find?

"Yeah, I got them," Wilbur said. "Here's one with two in it."

"Wilbur, I *got* that one! You're getting too close to me, I told you!"

They were near the northern end of the island. Anne pointed to some ducks swimming toward Gull Rock.

"Look, those are eiders," she said.

Roy looked through Anne's binoculars. "Yeah, sea ducks."

"Right—they're called eiders in the book."

"Well, I don't know," Roy said. "All I know is these old nicknames the lobster fishermen use."

"Come here!" Wilbur was shouting. "Here's *four!*"

Sure enough, Wilbur had discovered a nest with four eggs in it.

"I've *never* seen a tern's nest with four eggs," Anne said. "The book says it's very rare. This is really something. Usually three is the most. You'll have to make a special place in your notebooks."

But Roy had made a discovery, too. Nearby he saw an egg that seemed to move. Getting down on his hands and knees, he looked more closely.

"Here's an egg that's hatching!" he shouted.

Anne and the twins watched the tern chick chipping its way out of the egg. They could see it moving inside through its own square little window on the world.

"It will take a while," Anne said. "Let's remember where it is and come back later."

They went on with the count. When the boys had finished the area they had planned to cover, Anne told them to stop and add up their totals. They sat down on a rock and ate the two candy bars they had brought with them. Roy had listed 552 terns' eggs, Wilbur had 551.

"That's awfully close," Anne said. "I think any scientist would be satisfied with that kind of teamwork. We'll count the eggs in another area tomorrow."

"There's going to be a lot of little terns this year," Wilbur said.

"Well, not as many as you'd think from all the eggs," Anne said.

She pulled R. S. Palmer's book, *Maine Birds,* from a small canvas bag she had carried with her.

"Listen to this," she said, opening to the section on Arctic terns. "It says here that an ornithologist came out to this island in 1937. He made a study of one hundred terns' nests. He counted a hundred and forty-four eggs in those nests. Only ninety-one of the eggs hatched, and only twenty-three of them were still alive by the time they were old enough to fly."

"Gee, what happens to the chicks?" Wilbur asked.

"All kinds of things," Anne said. "If a spell of cold wet weather comes along while they're still very young, a lot of them will die. That's what happened in 1937. Then disease kills some. And gulls get others."

"So they have to lay a lot of eggs to make sure they get enough young birds," Roy said.

"Right," Anne said. "Now, let's go back and see if that chick has hacked its way out of the shell."

It had. When they reached the spot they found the egg lying in two pieces. Beside it, huddled under a clump of grass, was a tiny creature covered with

113

brownish fluff spotted in black. The fluff was still wet and matted. The chick had pink legs. At the end of its pink bill was a white egg tooth, so small the boys had to bend close to see it.

Roy reached out to touch the chick. The chick peeped and backed farther into the grass.

"We'd better leave it alone," Anne said. "It's liable to get scared away, and then its parents won't find it when they come back with food."

"I hope he lives," Roy said. He bent down again to look at the little creature huddled under the grass clump.

"So do I," Anne said.

Baby terns can walk and leave their nests within a few hours after hatching.

3

.

ONE MORNING ROY AND WILBUR LEARNED THAT THERE
were two sets of "strangers" on the island—strangers
to the boys, that is, but not to the island.

Anne told them about the first—a ghostly little bird
that came and went only at night. Though they had
walked all over the island and had watched
everything that moved, the twins had no idea that it
was there. They had, in a sense, been walking over
the bird. It was called a petrel. Dozens of them lived
in burrows dug in the soft earth among the weeds.

Rita Russell told them about the other "strangers."
They were a group of young bird students who had
been brought to the island by Captain Corbett early
in the morning. They had come to make a study of
the Arctic terns.

"Maybe we can help them," Roy said.

"Maybe we can," Anne said. "But first we have a
couple of studies of our own to finish."

It was a busy morning. They looked for puffin
chicks under the rocks and found four of them.
They counted the terns' eggs in a different area and
found 467 of them. They watched the gulls flying
over Gull Rock at the northern end of the island. Then
they went looking for a petrel.

Jack Russell suggested they look in the weeds at the northwestern end of the island.

"Watch out for the terns' eggs," Anne called as they walked through the weeds.

"Here's a hole!" Wilbur shouted.

He was already down on his hands and knees when Roy and Anne arrived. He stuck his arm into the narrow hole in the earth. He felt the hole bend. He reached around the corner, and his outstretched fingers touched a soft feathery something.

"I feel one," Wilbur said. His right side was already touching the ground as he reached to curl his fingers around the soft creature that struggled feebly to back away.

"Careful, don't squash it," Anne said.

"I'm being careful," Wilbur assured her. He had a grip on the bird now, and drew it slowly around the corner of the burrow and out into the daylight. The bird blinked, but did not try to escape. Roy and Anne moved in for a closer look.

It was a small, dusky, brownish black bird only eight inches long. Its eyes, bill, and webbed feet were black. There was nothing very special about the bird except its bill.

"Look at his bill," Wilbur said. "What's that?"

Wilbur had noticed a small tube running along the upper part of the bill.

"That funny-looking thing on its bill is the petrel's nostrils," Anne said. "They're in a little tube. The petrel spends all its life around the ocean. Scientists say the bird is able to take the salt out of the water it drinks, and get rid of it through those nostrils."

116

Wilbur reaches deep into a petrel burrow in the grassy area where these strange night-flying birds nest.

"He doesn't seem to be afraid of us," Roy said.

"No, I guess we're the first human beings it's ever seen. It doesn't know enough to be afraid of us. Petrels only come on land to nest, and they fly in and out of the burrows only at night. That's because they're not very fast flyers and the gulls can catch them in midair. They say even on a night of the full moon, when it's bright, the gulls catch a lot of petrels."

"It has a funny smell," Roy said.

Anne bent closer and sniffed the petrel's body. "Yes, it smells kind of musky. All petrels have that smell. It comes from some kind of oil they make in their stomachs to feed their chicks. People can sometimes find the burrows just by smelling them."

"Is this the chick?" Wilbur asked, looking at the bird in his hands.

"No, petrels are small birds to begin with," Anne told him. "Did you feel an egg down there?"

"I didn't notice," Wilbur said. "Here, hold him, and I'll find out."

He gave the petrel to Anne and stuck his arm down the hole again. A moment later he brought up a tiny white egg.

"There it is," he said, holding it up for them to see.

"Why isn't it speckled like the tern's egg?" Anne asked him.

Wilbur thought for a moment. "Oh—because it's always down there in the dark," he said. "There's no danger of the gulls seeing it when they fly overhead."

"Petrels are the birds that sailors call Mother Carey's chickens," Anne said. "They see them around boats all the time, flying low over the water and looking for tiny mollusks and fish on the water's surface. Sometimes they seem to be walking on the water. Some people say that's how they came to be called petrels—after Peter, who the Bible tells us walked on the water with Jesus' help."

"Look at his tiny feet," Roy said. "You wouldn't think he could dig a burrow with those feet."

"No, you wouldn't," Anne said. "Petrels' feet are so tiny that they have trouble walking on them, and they use their wings like crutches to help themselves move on land. But they use their feet and their bills to dig their burrows. That's why they usually nest in soft spongy earth. Okay, time to put the petrel back."

Wilbur reached down the burrow to set the egg back where he had found it. Then Anne put the petrel into the hole and covered the opening for a few seconds with her hand.

"We don't want the petrel to get confused and fly out again," she explained. "The gulls might catch it."

They began to walk along the rocks toward the blinds.

"The gulls cause a lot of trouble, don't they?" Roy asked.

"Well, the gulls have been living alongside these birds for thousands of years, and these seabirds have done all right," Anne said. "The trouble is that man has made life easy for the gulls because of his garbage dumps. Gulls find what they want to eat around dumps. They grow happy and healthy and their population has increased.

Looking sinister, a herring gull prowls the rocks looking for tern chicks left unguarded by their parents.

"Then the gulls come back to these islands every year to nest. There are many more of them than there used to be. But there are no garbage dumps around these islands where they can get food for themselves and their young. So some of them eat a lot of the other birds' eggs and chicks."

Near the whistle house they saw four young men and a girl, the people Captain Corbett had brought over earlier in the morning.

"Can we go over and see what they're doing?" Wilbur asked.

Anne told them to go ahead. The boys learned that the newcomers were making a study for the Massachusetts Audubon Society. Their leader was Jeremy, a young Englishman, and they were fashioning simple traps out of chicken wire in order to catch terns.

"Can we help?" Wilbur asked.

"Sure," Jeremy said.

He showed them how to cut the chicken wire and shape it. He bent the sides down so that they formed a box without a top. When a number of traps were ready, they picked them up and carried them into the weeds where there were many terns' nests.

"Why are you going to catch terns?" Roy asked.

Jeremy explained that another Englishman had banded Arctic terns on this island and several other islands off the Maine coast twenty-two years before. Until recently no one had known whether many terns lived to be twenty years old or more, as gulls often do. But now several terns had been found wearing the bands that the Englishman had put on them so many years before.

Wilbur helps one of the visiting Audubon researchers catch terns for banding.

"So we want to see if we can capture some more of these terns that have the old bands on," Jeremy said. "We've already caught some on another island. This is very exciting because sand and salt water break down the bands after a while and many of them fall off. Since we've already caught a number of these old birds, it probably means there are a lot more of them around, but their bands have fallen off."

Jeremy told them where to set traps. Then he went back to the oil shed where he was getting ready to put new bands on the legs of all the terns they caught.

Roy and Wilbur helped the others to set the traps. They took the stem of an angelica plant and used it to prop up the chicken wire trap over a set of eggs. They always made sure to set up the trap's opening away from the wind because terns land by flying into the wind, and that is the way they would approach their nests.

Then the boys and the Audubon people walked out onto the rocks and waited for the terns to come back to their nests.

"Here comes one now," Wilbur said.

Everyone watched very carefully. The tern landed and walked over to its nest. It paid no attention to the chicken wire trap over the eggs. It walked right to the eggs and knocked the stem out from under the trap with its tail. The trap fell down and the tern was caught under it.

"The chicken wire is very light and it doesn't hurt the tern," one of the young men said.

They waited until eight terns had been caught in this way. Then everybody went to work. Jeremy had

given them several white pillowcases. Each pillowcase
had had four or five pockets sewn into the inside of it.
Roy and Wilbur helped take the terns out of the
traps and stuff them into the pockets in the
pillowcases. Then Roy carried all the pillowcases up
to the oil shed, while Wilbur helped the others to
set up the traps again.

Roy totes two sacks of terns to the banding station.

Jeremy, an English ornithologist making a study for the Massachusetts Audubon Society, bands, measures, and weighs a tern while Roy watches.

Banded Arctic terns have been found to live for over twenty years.

Roy watched Jeremy as he banded the terns. The young Englishman took a tern out of a pillowcase, smoothed its ruffled feathers, measured its wings with a ruler, and weighed it on a small scale. The tern took Jeremy's index finger in its bill.

"Doesn't it hurt?" Roy asked.

"No, terns don't bite hard like puffins do," Jeremy said.

He took a tiny aluminum band from a box and slipped it on the tern's leg. Then he tightened the band with a small pincers. In a notebook that he kept beside him he wrote down the date and place where the bird had been captured, its weight and measurements, and the number of the band he had put on its leg.

"This one's ready to go home," Jeremy said.

He took the tern outside the building and opened his hands. For a moment the bird could not believe its good fortune. Then it realized it was free to go, flapped its wings, and took off. Jeremy came back in the building and began to band another tern.

"We've been counting their eggs," Roy said.

"Oh, yes? Did you count very many?"

"Quite a few," Roy said. "My brother and I have got the number written down in our notebooks. We found four eggs in one nest."

"You did?" Jeremy looked interested. "Four, you say? That's *very* unusual. Arctic terns almost never lay four eggs."

"What do you think it is, then?" Roy asked.

Jeremy shrugged. "Perhaps it's a common tern."

"Can we put a trap over it and find out?" Roy asked.

"Sure," Jeremy said. "Show us where the nest is, and we'll see if we can catch the bird."

The boys spent a long afternoon helping the Audubon party to trap and band the terns. They admired the way Jeremy handled the struggling birds, working carefully so that he would not injure their fragile-looking wings. Later they sat on the rocks, watching the puffins fly in from the sea. Anne came over to see how they were doing.

"Roy and Wilbur are good workers," Jeremy told her. "They've helped us a lot."

"Was the banding a success?" Anne asked him.

"Yes," he said. "We got several more of the old birds. We've always known, of course, that not many of the terns lived to be one year old. In fact, probably fewer do now than before because the gulls are pretty bad on some of the islands we've visited. Here the gulls are not so bad because they're afraid of the lighthouse keepers, and don't come over so often to catch the terns' chicks. But I would hate to see what might happen if the lighthouse keepers left this island.

"In any case, we're proving that once the Arctic tern gets past that first year it's got a chance to live for a long time."

"We set a trap at the nest that has the four eggs," Roy told Anne.

"Oh—what happened?"

"Well, we caught an Arctic tern," Jeremy said. "But I'm still not convinced that one tern laid all those eggs. Sometimes two females lay eggs in the same nest. I would guess that's what happened here."

"I used to think, when I was in school, that scientists had answered all the questions about nature," Anne said. "But the more you learn, the more you know how much there still is for us to find out."

"That's right," Jeremy said. "If boys like Roy and Wilbur want to become scientists, there will always be lots of problems for them to solve."

4

·

THE BOYS' LAST FULL DAY ON THE ISLAND WAS DRAWING
to a close. The puffins were flying in from the
darkening sea to spend an hour or two loafing on the
rocks before night fell. The boys sat on the front steps
of the Russells' house. A tree swallow flew back and
forth over the grass, snapping up insects. Its mate sat
quietly on the roof of a small birdhouse that the
Russells had set up on a pole.

"We've got some tree swallows at home," Wilbur
said. "I wonder why they stop on this little island."

"There are quite a few land birds here," Anne said.
"How many have you seen?"

Wilbur pulled his notebook out of his pocket.

"Well—I saw tree swallows . . . barn swallows . . .
a sparrow . . . a redwing blackbird . . . and a blue jay."

"No woodpeckers?" Anne asked, smiling.

Wilbur grinned too. "No woodpeckers. There's
no trees here for them to peck."

"But there are *tree* swallows."

"That's because the Russells put up that
birdhouse," Wilbur said.

"And the barn swallows nest around the oil shed,"
Roy said. "It looks something like a barn anyway. I
guess if there weren't any people here, or any
buildings, birds like that wouldn't stop here."

130

This tree swallow's house has been blown cockeyed by the strong ocean winds.

"That's right," Anne said. "There wouldn't be any nesting place to attract them. But the birds themselves supply some of the nesting places around here. Can you think of any?"

The twins liked this kind of talk. It was like a jigsaw puzzle—putting all the pieces together to form a picture of the island that made sense. They looked around them.

"A lot of birds nest in the weeds," Roy said. "The books say that sometimes birds eat weed seeds in one place, and drop them later on someplace else. Maybe that's how these weeds got here to begin with. The birds dropped the seeds."

Anne nodded. "Maybe so," she said.

"Then the birds helped make this island look the way it does today," Wilbur added.

Anne nodded again. "That's one of the things that did it. The sea made the island in the first place when it rose and filled up all the valleys, and left only the mountaintops sticking out.

"Then some seeds and tiny plants were washed up on the shore here by the waves. Maybe the wind carried some seeds here from the mainland, too. And maybe people brought weed seeds here, mixed in with the seeds for flowers and vegetables they wanted to plant. They probably kept a cow out here for milk in the old days, and maybe there were seeds in its feed. The seeds grew to be plants. So the birds saw plant life here and came to feed on it. And maybe they brought other seeds with them."

They could see the puffins now standing in groups on the rocks. From a distance the birds looked like crowds of people standing on sidewalks and chatting with their friends.

"Over there are other things that aren't cut off from what happens someplace else," Anne said, pointing to the puffins. "For a while the puffins were increasing their numbers. But now all the oil spills from tankers seem to be having an effect on them. The ocean is full of oil. And the oil is killing thousands of puffins and razorbills—birds that spend so much time swimming on the water."

"Could they become extinct?" Roy asked.

"Well, there seem to be enough of them. But in the last century even the ornithologists thought there were enough great auks around so that they wouldn't become extinct. Even after the great auk became extinct, people thought for a while some more might be discovered in the far north. But it was too late."

"Between the gulls and the oil, these birds have a hard time," Roy said.

"Man makes the garbage dumps that mean more gulls," Anne said. "And he spills the oil that pollutes the ocean. Well, it's almost petrel time. Let's get ready."

It had grown dark. Anne and the boys put on heavy jackets to guard against the night chill. Then they took flashlights and went over to the rocks close to the petrel burrows. This was their last chance to see the petrels coming and going at night.

"Gee, the terns never shut up, do they?" Wilbur said.

The terns still flew overhead, keeping the night alive with their cries. Across the island, the beam from the lighthouse shone out over the water. But the rocks where the boys sat were covered in darkness.

"There goes something—I think," Wilbur said.

"I didn't see anything," Roy said.

They sat in silence for a few minutes more.

"There goes something!" Roy whispered.

"I didn't see anything," Wilbur said.

It was difficult to make out the forms in the darkness. The wind rustled the weeds behind them. The terns flew noisily overhead.

"There's something!" Wilbur said.

"I saw it, too," Roy agreed.

This drawing by Guy Coheleach shows a petrel in flight over the water. A drawing is necessary because of the difficulty in photographing these night-flying creatures.

They had seen a little form dart past them that time. It had come from the sea. A moment later another form flew past. And then another, fluttering like a bat in the dark, but clearly larger.

They were in the middle of the mysterious nighttime world of the petrels. Once in a while they heard a thin peep. Petrels were coming in from the sea to relieve their mates who had been waiting patiently for them, perhaps for several days. The hungry birds, freed of the task of sitting on the single white egg down in the darkness of the burrow, flew quickly out to sea.

After a while, it became too chilly to stay out of doors, and Anne and the boys made their way back in the darkness to the house and their warm beds. But for a little while they had been part of a world so secret that few people even know that it exists.

The boys awoke with a start. The foghorn had sounded in the night. Its blast—the long groan and the short grunt—was loud and strange, startling even the terns into a moment of silence. Their island—the boys had come to think of it after only a few days as *their* island—seemed smaller and lonelier than ever. Tomorrow they would be going home.

They lay awake, unable to sleep. DAN-GER! the foghorn seemed to be saying. The island was not really cut off from the rest of the world, even in the thick fog. It was telling the world something.

During their five days on the island the twins had come to see that no part of the natural world is cut off from another. The seed that a bird picks up on the

135

Dense fog shrouds the island as the beams of the lighthouse circle continuously to warn ships at sea.

mainland may someday sprout a flower on *this* island. The shortening of daylight in another hemisphere will send a beautiful seabird ten thousand miles to produce a downy little chick on *this* island. The oil that someone spills from a ship halfway around the world thins out the numbers of puffins on *this* island.

"Captain Corbett's got to come and get us in the fog," Wilbur said.

"Yeah," Roy said. "But the fog didn't bother us any while we were here. We were lucky."

"We were lucky," Wilbur agreed. He was silent for a moment. Then he said, "Yes. We were lucky."

BOOKS ABOUT SEABIRDS

These are the books that Roy and Wilbur
brought with them to the island.

A Field Guide to the Birds, by Roger Tory Peterson. Boston, 1947.
Life Histories of North American Diving Birds, by Arthur C. Bent.
Washington, D.C., 1919.
Life Histories of North American Gulls and Terns, by Arthur C.
Bent. Washington, D.C., 1921.
Maine Birds, by Ralph S. Palmer. Cambridge, Mass., 1949.
Puffins, by R. M. Lockley. Garden City, N.Y., 1962.

NOTE: All of these books, except *Maine Birds,* are available in
paperback editions.

ABOUT THE AUTHORS:

Ada and Frank Graham, Jr., have written a number of highly
successful books about conservation and ecology, including a recent
Cowles juvenile, *Wildlife Rescue: Alternative to Extinction.* Mr.
Graham, a field editor for *Audubon Magazine,* is also the author
of last season's critically acclaimed *Since Silent Spring.*

ABOUT THE PHOTOGRAPHER:

Les Line is editor-in-chief of *Audubon,* the magazine of the National
Audubon Society. He is also well known for his photography, which
has appeared in many books, magazines, and calendars. He is
currently working on several books, including *The World of the
Nature Photographer* and a full-color photographic guide to the
wild flowers of eastern North America.

138

INDEX

Page numbers in italics refer to illustrations.

J 598.2
Graham
Puffin Island

34,236

WITHDRAWN

Return this book on or before the last
date stamped below

DEC 15 '71	SEP 21 '79	NOV 28 1983	AUG 2 1988
JAN 10 '72	JUL 14 1980	MAR 22 1984	AUG 16 1988
FEB 23 73	DEC 3 1980	APR 10 1984	AUG 23 1988
JUL 30 74	AUG 3 1981	APR 10 1985	JUN 2 1988
APR 14 '75	AUG 12 1981	DEC 2 1985	
MAY 22 '75	FEB 13 1982	FEB 9 1987	
JUN 4 '76			
JUN 3 77			
AUG 4 '77			
NOV 3 '77	OCT	FEB 1983	
FEB 15 '78			
FEB 7 '79	OCT 11 1983		
FEB 10 '79			
JUL 26 '79			

Library Bureau Cat. No. 1174